T0373434

Life, in Pictures

The Will Eisner Library

from W. W. Norton & Company

Hardcover Compilations

The Contract With God *Trilogy: Life on Dropsie Avenue*
Will Eisner's New York: Life in the Big City

Paperbacks

A Contract With God
A Life Force
Dropsie Avenue
New York: The Big City
City People Notebook
Will Eisner Reader
The Dreamer
Invisible People
To the Heart of the Storm
Life on Another Planet
Family Matter
Minor Miracles
The Name of the Game
The Building
The Plot: The Secret History of the Protocols of the Elders of Zion

Instructional Textbooks

Comics and Sequential Art
Graphic Storytelling
Expressive Anatomy

Other Books by Will Eisner

Fagin the Jew
Last Day in Vietnam
Eisner/Miller
The Spirit Archives
Will Eisner Sketchbook
Will Eisner's Shop Talk
Hawks of the Seas
The Princess and the Frog
The Last Knight
Moby Dick
Sundiata

Life, in Pictures

Autobiographical
Stories

Will Eisner

W. W. NORTON & COMPANY
New York • London

Copyright © 2007 by Will Eisner Studios, Inc.
Introduction by Scott McCloud copyright © 2007 by Scott McCloud

"A Sunset in Sunshine City" copyright © 1985 by Will Eisner
The·Dreamer copyright © 1986 by Will Eisner
To the Heart of the Storm copyright © 1991 by Will Eisner
The Name of the Game copyright © 2001 by Will Eisner
"The Day I Became a Professional" copyright © 2003 by Will Eisner. "The Day I
Became a Professional" included with the permission of Will Eisner Studios, Inc.

All rights reserved
Printed in the United States of America
First Edition

For information about permission to reproduce
selections from this book, write to Permissions,
W. W. Norton & Company, Inc.
500 Fifth Avenue, New York, NY 10110

For information about special discounts for bulk purchases,
please contact W. W. Norton Special Sales at
specialsales@wwnorton.com or 800-233-4830

Manufacturing by RR Donnelley, Willard
Production manager: Julia Druskin

Library of Congress Cataloging-in-Publication Data

Eisner, Will.
Life, in pictures : autobiographical stories / Will Eisner.
p. cm.
ISBN 978-0-393-06107-9 (hardcover)
1. Eisner, Will—Comic books, strips, etc. 2. Cartoonists—
United States—Biography—Comic books, strips, etc.
I. Title.
PN6727.E4Z46 2007
741.5'973—dc22
[B]
2007032339

W. W. Norton & Company, Inc.
500 Fifth Avenue, New York, N.Y. 10110
www.wwnorton.com

W. W. Norton & Company Ltd.
Castle House, 75/76 Wells Street, London W1T 3QT

1 2 3 4 5 6 7 8 9 0

Contents

Introduction

A Will to Change

I saw Will Eisner for the last time in early October 2004 in his spacious, well-organized office and drawing studio, nestled among the accountants, realtors and dentists of sunny Tamarac, Florida. At eighty-seven years old, the man was as young-hearted and energetic as ever, showing me plans and drawings for upcoming projects, sharing funny anecdotes with my awestruck traveling companion, refusing to let me pay for lunch at a nearby family restaurant. Two months later, in a hotel in Boston, I pulled up a photo I'd taken that October day and was puzzled to find an old man's face on my computer screen—deeply lined, unrecognizable—a pixilated Dorian Gray. Clearly, my camera didn't know him as I did. Still, I wondered if there would ever come a time when I'd begin to see my mentor the same way, as an old man. Later that day, the phone rang, and a mutual friend told me that Will Eisner had died the previous evening, January 3, 2005.

Will Eisner may have lived to the ripe old age of eighty-seven, but to this day there are comics artists, myself included, who insist that he died before his time. In our strange reckoning, a mere quadruple bypass operation shouldn't have cost him more than a day or two. We shake our heads a little every time we think of the day we heard the news, brows furrowed, working on an unsolved problem. After all these years, wasn't he just getting started?

Our society expects the story of each human life to have a beginning, middle and ending, but Eisner knew that nothing ever ends; that our lives can be a cascade of new beginnings if we have the wit and will to make it so. We can see it in the stories of *Life, in Pictures*; how the quiet remembrance of the past that opens "A Sunset in Sunshine City" does nothing to slow the pace of change in the world; how the new medium and industry seen in *The Dreamer* could be set in motion from the humblest of beginnings. And we see it especially in the man himself; how he never lost faith in comics' ability to grow and mature, even during periods when comics in America looked as dead as a week-old cadaver to everyone else.

Will was already a legend in the industry and literally three times my age when I met him in 1982, but in the twenty-five years that followed, I was constantly struck by how often he seemed the youngest man in the room. Whether defending the honor of "amateurish junk" to publishers and pundits arguing for its suppression in the mid-1990s, or defending new visions of comics to his uncomprehending peers, comics' "grand old man" was frequently cast in the role of the young turk, stubbornly banging on the door of status quo thinking.

Even I—comics' so-called "futurist"—found myself in the role of the stubborn old man over dinner one night, trying to talk Will out of starting an online comics school because I thought the Web was still too primitive for what he had in mind. He often joked about McCloud "hitting me over the head with a Wacom tablet, telling me to get in tune with the future!" but here I was, cast in the role of *Luddite*, telling the wide-eyed young futurist "it'll never work."

Will never stood on ceremony. I was expected to call him by his first name as we all were. None of his ideas were too sacred to be challenged. None of ours were too strange or new to be considered. He thrived on the debates of the young and, speaking on behalf of the young (I'm a mere forty-six as I write this, barely out of diapers), we were happy and honored to have him at the table. But it was more than just personal disposition that drove him to seek out new ideas. It was also his mature understanding of the nature of comics itself, and how malleable a form it could be.

Eisner—like the giants of film, prose and theater—refused to buy into the myth of manifest destiny; that comforting but specious assumption that the popular storytelling conventions of our day are just an inevitable offspring of time, place and the tools of the trade. He knew that the lives of art forms aren't drawn by fate at all, but by the arbitrary paths of creative individuals. While "comics historians" celebrated comics' beginnings only to the extent that they paved the way for the present they knew, Eisner saw the galaxy of roads not taken, the stories we might have read but couldn't because their authors were never encouraged, never hired or simply never born. And he saw *new* roads leading to a drastically altered landscape for his chosen art, the landscape we can see springing up around us today.

When you enter a "graphic novels" section of a bookstore, you're looking at Will's handiwork, a vision he saw as clearly over twenty-five years ago. When you see the whole page considered as a unit in modern comics, you're experiencing an aesthetic echo of work done by Will over sixty-five years ago. When industry figures and artists break bread and apply themselves toward common causes in a spirit of collegiality, they're walking down a path Will walked throughout his career.

The Will I knew was all these things, but I won't kid myself that I knew the whole man. When attending his memorial in March of 2005 in a deconsecrated synagogue in Manhattan's Lower East Side, I heard peers make jokes about how "cheap" their old buddy was, while simultaneously praising his humanitarian side—two qualities that never surfaced in all my encounters with him. I never saw him play tennis (he was good!). I never saw him making business deals. And I never once heard Will or his wife, Ann, mention the central tragedy of their life—the death of their only daughter, Alice.

Here in this collection are aspects of the Will Eisner I didn't know: The prejudice that he endured, and the calamitous worldwide changes that invade his dreams in *To the Heart of the Storm*; the bitter, desperate side of human nature that he bears witness to in *The Name of the Game* and "A Sunset in Sunshine City"; the early days of the comics industry and its denizens brought to life in *The Dreamer* and "The Day I Became a Professional." There's so much of the man that I never saw, but what I did see altered my outlook on life and art, and that outlook altered everything that followed.

When I consider how to spend the next forty years of my productive life, I'm on Will Eisner's timetable. When I seek out artists half my age to learn my craft, I'm following Will Eisner's playbook. When I see comics as a blank slate, able to accommodate any idea, any style, any level of creative endeavor, I'm looking through Will Eisner's lens. My peers and I were as much his medium as the paper and ink he wielded with such authority. He changed comics not only through his work, but also through the changes brought about by those *he* changed from generation to generation.

You may hear an industry pundit or two claim that thanks to Will Eisner, comics have finally "arrived," and so they have, but only in the sense of a train arriving at a station, pausing for a few minutes only, while its late conductor's children frantically lay new tracks toward his cherished horizon.

Scott McCloud
February 2007

Editor's Note

As Will Eisner himself often noted, he "did not invent comic books, but was present at their birth." Shortly out of high school, in the mid-1930s, he was already contributing to some of the earliest American comic books. And, remarkably, while still a teenager, he cofounded Eisner & Iger Studios, which quickly became a major comic book packaging house. There he both created comics and employed many of the industry's brightest talents. But Eisner & Iger's publishing customers were interested solely in commercial products: formulaic costumed heroes and adventure comics aimed at a young male market hungry for a steady diet of cheap four-color escapism.

Eisner next moved to a syndicated masked hero. *The Spirit*, launched in 1940 as a Sunday newspaper insert, was innovative both in format and in storytelling techniques. Eisner had considerably more creative freedom with *The Spirit* (a property he also owned) and he occasionally worked himself—or a cartoonist stand-in—into storylines. In one particularly memorable such *Spirit* story, in late 1950, Eisner was killed by his then-assistant Jules Feiffer, who proceeded to take over the strip. But truly autobiographical comics were out of the question during Eisner's formative comic book years, as they were for any cartoonist toiling in the industry during its first four decades.

This compilation, the last of three hardcovers in the Will Eisner Library, focuses on the autobiographical portion of Will Eisner's graphic novels, though it does not represent the entirety of such works. Elements of *A Contract With God* in W. W. Norton's initial Eisner trilogy are autobiographical as well. Eisner drew from personal experiences in many of his stories but he avoided pure autobiography until quite late in his career. Auteur cartoonists—half artist and half writer—do not enjoy the long traditions of their literary cousins. And even Eisner, a lifelong innovator, who pioneered the graphic novel genre in the last phase of his long career, was influenced late on, as he often acknowledged, by a younger generation of "underground" cartoonists, who broke many of the conventional rules of the comic genre beginning in the late 1960s. Eisner, who saw his first underground comix in the summer of 1971, was impressed and inspired by the young artists' complete artistic freedom, along with the autobiographical nature of certain works by cartoonists like Robert Crumb and Justin Green.

Responding to this influence, Eisner first tackled autobiographical topics in his groundbreaking *A Contract With God* in 1978. In the opening scenes of the title story, a weeping Frimme Hersh, in a torrential rain, returns from burying his young daughter. Eisner publicly confessed in 2004 that this premise was based on the early death of his only daughter, Alice, a life shattering experience for him and his wife, Ann. While the remainder of this story is fictional, the lead character's profound break with God over the violation of an innate "contract" parallels Eisner's own struggles to comprehend a caring deity following Alice's death. Of the other stories in *A Contract With God*, only "Cookalein" is comprised of autobiographical elements, with the key clue being the young man named "Willie."

It would be a number of years before Eisner chose to return to autobiographical themes. Five distinct pieces make up this *Life, in Pictures* collection. The title of the compilation is not predicated by "A" or "My" because while three of the five elements are truly autobiographical, another is largely biographical (Ann's family) and a fifth reflects a significant shift in Eisner's life but is not his personal story. We present the stories here not in the chronological order of the events depicted but, rather, in the order in which Eisner created them.

After being born, living and working for their entire lives, aside from Will's army years, in greater New York City, Ann and Will moved to Florida in 1984. Uprooting from his beloved New York was not an easy adjustment and the cartoonist dealt with it in part by creating "A Sunset in Sunshine City" in 1985. (It first appeared in *Will Eisner's Quarterly* #6, and then in *Will Eisner Reader*.) The story is clearly fictional, but the retiring Henry Klop is an entrepreneurial New Yorker roughly Will's own age at the time the story was created. The family and business memories flooding back as Henry surveys his old neighborhood in a driving snow are no doubt a reflection of Eisner's own bittersweet feelings, while some of Klop's Florida experiences are a very real reflection of Eisner's own culture shock. And when Henry expresses resistance to a boring, monotonous retirement, he appears to foreshadow Eisner's first major autobiographical work when he says, "Living for tomorrow has been my life . . . Always dreams, Rita . . . *Dreams!*"

The Dreamer (1986), which follows "A Sunset in Sunshine City," tells the story of an idealistic young artist's entry into the rapidly mushrooming comic book business prior to World War II. The young artist, Billy, is, of course, Eisner, and the succession of professionals he encounters are also real, but all players and entities are given thinly disguised pseudonyms in this engaging roman à clef. Some of Will's associates during the creation of this story, myself included, urged him to flesh this story out, to name names, to expand the characterizations and story, especially the scandalous elements, and to create, in essence, *Will Eisner's Personal History of Comics.* But this is the more compact story he wanted to tell. For any reader who would like help identifying the various historic figures and companies appearing in *The Dreamer,* annotations follow the story.

Eisner's most overtly autobiographical work is *To the Heart of the Storm* (1990), an ambitious undertaking more than four times the length of *The Dreamer.* A uniformed Eisner, sitting on a troop train in 1942, frames the individual stories in *Heart.* As he looks pensively out the train window, the rapidly moving images merge into flashbacks. This time actual names are used and personal experiences and family lore are shown in considerable detail. The depicted events are not chronological. Stories of Eisner's own childhood and youth are interspersed with those of his parents and grandparents. What all the generations commonly share in these stories are bitter encounters with prejudice against Jews. *To the Heart of the Storm* is as much a story of anti-Semitism as it is autobiography.

Having told his early entrepreneurial history in *The Dreamer* and his own family's history in *To the Heart of the Storm*, Eisner then turned his attention to Ann's family in *The Name of the Game* (2001). Eisner here adroitly combines actual persons and events with fiction. The autocratic Conrad Arnheim is based on Ann's father, who in real life, like Arnheim, inherited a once highly successful corset manufacturing company and was a well-connected stockbroker. Most primary events, even the dramatic kidnapping scene, are reality based. Arnheim's last daughter Rosie is based on Ann, and thus Aron the poet, Rosie's eventual husband, is, loosely speaking, Eisner himself. Aron's off-the-boat blue-collar parents and the aristocratic Arnheims, other than sharing a Jewish heritage, have nothing whatever in common, closely paralleling their real-life counterparts. Eisner takes the greatest liberty with his own character. Ann's father wanted his new son-in-law to join his brokerage firm and in real life Will declined, in order to continue pursuing his own career in publishing. But in *The Name of the Game* Eisner takes the literary opportunity to play "what if" and casts himself unsympathetically as a poet who evolves into an avaricious and self-centered businessman who callously cheats on his wife (becoming in effect the new Conrad).

The very last autobiographical piece Eisner created, in 2003, ironically depicts one of the earliest moments in his career. Only four pages in length, "The Day I Became a Professional" appeared in Dark Horse Comics' *AutobioGraphix* anthology and harkens back to Eisner's portfolio-carrying dreamer.

Eisner's depictions of himself, family members and friends are usually not sparing in warts, but he stopped short at truly intimate detail. While underground comix influenced his decision to explore autobiography, and he appreciated the graphic intensity, private revelations and sometimes sexually explicit nature of the undergrounds, he made no effort to compete with them on an earthy level. This relative restraint reflected both the generational and gentlemanly side of Eisner. As he once noted, using hippie vernacular, "I can't let it all hang out like Crumb." Eisner's candor was expressed in other manners. For example, while there were surely "dreamer" aspects to Eisner, as with virtually every artist, he was also an exceptionally astute businessman, something quite rare among artists of all generations. That very pragmatic and even shrewd side of Eisner allowed him to plausibly play out the role of poet-turned-amoral-businessman in *The Name of the Game*, territory that would be alien to nearly any other cartoonist, including the normally fearless Crumb.

Being a product of the Great Depression, a New York Jew, a workaholic loner and a self-made man were all characteristics reflected strongly in his work, both autobiographical and fictional, and are critical to understanding Eisner the man, but they could be ascribed to most of the numerous other cartoonists of his era. What differentiated Will Eisner from his contemporaries was what he called his "literary pretensions." At the age of twenty-four, long before comic books and strips were taken seriously, even by the most successful of his fellow professionals, he showed remarkable prescience. In a 1941 newspaper article, Eisner boldly stated that comics were the "embryo of a new art form . . . an illustrated novel. It is new and raw in form just now, but material for limitless intelligent development. And eventually and inevitably it will be a legitimate medium for the best of writers and artists." For more than six decades after articulating this vision of comics' literary and artistic potential, Eisner demonstrated firsthand what was possible, establishing the first beachhead, and inspiring countless other artists, in what is now a recognized literary genre.

Denis Kitchen
Amherst, Massachusetts
November 2006

Life, in Pictures

27

31

34

37

41

43

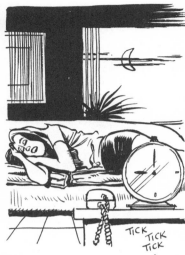

OH, WELL, HENRY, YOU MIGHT AS WELL KNOW IT NOW!! JERRY AND I... **WE'RE GETTING MARRIED!**

YEAH,...AS SOON AS MY DIVORCE FROM RITA COMES THROUGH! I FILED IT LAST WEEK!

I KNOW IT'S VERY SUDDEN, BUT IN THE LAST MONTH JERRY HAS SHOWN ME I'M STILL A YOUNG WOMAN...AND FRANKLY, TO TIE MYSELF DOWN TO AN **OLDER** MAN IS FOOLISH...I'M SURE YOU UNDERSTAND!

HE'S A **BUM!** OLGA, HE CAN'T MAKE A LIVING!

NOT TO WORRY, MY HUSBAND, TONY, LEFT ME **VERY** WELL PROVIDED FOR.

I WON'T NEED TO WAIT AROUND FOR **YOUR** INHERITANCE! OLGA BELIEVES IN MY DEAL... SHE'LL **BACK** ME!

IT'S NOT THE END OF THE WORLD, HENRY!

YOU STILL HAVE **YOUR** DAUGHTER TO LOOK AFTER YOU.

TICK TICK

TICK TICK   TICK TICK

TICK TICK TICK

VITAM

TICK TICK TICK TICK

48

THE DREAMER

Introduction to
The Dreamer

At best, society tends to regard its dreamers with tolerance.

Dreamers journey through life to a cadence all their own. They make decisions or enter undertakings that often seem naive and confounding to the pragmatists, who, in the end, thrive on opportunities set in motion by fantasy and imaginings. This is a story about a dreamer. It is a walk alongside a young cartoonist on the threshold of his career. It is an examination of hope and ambition. The events take place during a time when cartoonists found themselves on fallow ground, the dawn of the modern comic book industry during the mid-1930s.

It was a very special era. Young cartoonists struggling to enter the established markets had come upon a new opportunity—the comic book medium. Here was a publishing format, actually a mutant grown out of Sunday newspaper comic sections, that welcomed innovation and was wide open to newcomers. Standards were still quite low—as were the prices paid for pages.

In this mini-frontier, many new comic book production studios suddenly appeared and prospered almost overnight. In this workshops cartoonists, illustrators and writers worked long hours, propelled by their dreams . . . many of which would surely come true someday. From these eager young talents came the great comic book heroes that are still viable after almost five decades.

Today the comic book art form is beginning to find critical acceptance as a respectable popular literature, and many of these creators, internationally recognized at last, are enjoying the fruits of having "arrived." But in the early years, they were not much different from their modern successors who still struggle with similar aspirations, but in an already established field.

The big difference, perhaps, is the fact that they lived back then in a magical time, unmindful that the anecdotes they spun and the legends they made would, one day, become part of the lore of the comic books' beginnings.

The Dreamer, intended as a work of fiction, ultimately took on the shape of a historical account. In the telling, it was inescapable that the actors would resemble real people. Their names, however, are fictitious, and they are portrayed without malice. It all comes out of the cluttered closet where I store ghosts of the past, and from the yellowing memories of my experience.

Will Eisner
1986
Florida

The Dreamer is based on Will Eisner's personal experiences in the comics industry. For readers who would like help identifying the various historic figures and companies that appear here, annotations follow on pages 99–104.

...IT'S ON THE THIRD FLOOR... ONLY $10 A MONTH...WITH A TWO-MONTH CONCESSION..., SOME WEIRD BUSINESSES IN THE BUILDING!! THEY TAKE SHORT LEASES, JIMMY!

GOOD! I DON'T KNOW HOW LONG WE CAN HOLD OUT!

...NOT MUCH ROOM IN HERE.*

OH, IT'S ENOUGH FOR A **BOARD** AND A DESK...YOU'LL BE OUT SELLING MOST OF THE TIME.

...NO, MOMMA, I'LL BE HERE WORKING ALL NIGHT...GOT A DEADLINE!

?!

"I TELL YOU...PINKY BLUE" IN THE FOURTH

WE GOT IT WIRED!! IT'S A SURE SHOT

...GOOD NEWS, JIM! LAST NIGHT I OVER-HEARD THE BOOKIE NEXT DOOR FIX THE FOURTH RACE AT YONKERS...SO, I PUT ALL OUR PETTY CASH ON "PINKY BLUE" TO WIN!

REALLY?

IF WE CAN'T DO IT IN COMICS, MAYBE WE CAN MAKE IT ON THE PONIES!

SHHH THE RADIO IS ON!

...AND IT'S....LEFTY LOU IN THE FOURTH

WRONG HORSE!! OKAY, DREAMER, BACK TO THE DRAWING BOARD!

67

MOST OF THE COMICS BEING OFFERED ARE JUST **IMITATIONS** OF THE DAILY NEWSPAPER STRIPS. HERE ARE SOME...THEY'RE ADVENTURE STRIPS... COWBOY, DETECTIVE AND HUMOR... I THINK YOU SHOULD STICK WITH THESE ADVENTURE STORIES!

I SEE...LOTS OF ACTION, EH??

RIGHT!! KIDS BUY THESE TEN CENT BOOKS! SO, WE SHOULD HAVE LOTS OF ACTION, EH?

"...WHAT ELSE YOU GOT, MAXWELL?

...AND THIS IS A STRIP CALLED "**BIG HERO**" BY TWO KIDS FROM OHIO!

YOU CAN BUY THIS STUFF EASY...THEY BEEN TURNED DOWN BY EVERYONE IN TOWN!

WE'LL PAY 7 BUCKS A PAGE.

OKAY, BUT HOW DO WE PUT THIS STUFF TOGETHER?

I'LL HELP UNTIL YOU GET ROLLING.

SOME DAY SOON... I'LL PUT OUT MY OWN BOOKS...

OKAY, WE'VE GOT 64 PAGES OF STUFF... WE'LL CALL IT BANG COMICS!!

MAKE SURE TO PROTECT OUR OWNERSHIP! STAMP "FOR ALL RIGHTS AND TITLE" ON THE BACK OF EACH CHECK WE PAY OUT!

"...ALMOST A YEAR SINCE WE STARTED UP, BILLY!"

WITH THE NEW CUSTOMERS I GOT THIS MONTH, WE'RE MAKING MONEY. EVEN AT $5 A PAGE WE'LL NET OVER $10,000 THIS YEAR ... NOT BAD!

YES, BUT IT'S GETTING HARDER TO HOLD ONTO OUR FREE-LANCERS

HYA BILLY, JIMMY.

HI, CORN.* WE'VE BEEN WAITING FOR YOUR STUFF ..Y'R LATE!

THIS IS THE LAST "PUPPY DAWG" PAGE I'M DOING FOR YOU GUYS!

WHY?!

I SOLD "RODENTMAN," MY COSTUME HERO, TO HARRIFIELD...AND THEY'RE PAYING ME $7 A PAGE!

JEEZ, WE CAN'T MEET THAT PRICE.

SEE YA, GUYS!

I SEE WHAT YOU MEAN...OKAY, THERE AREN'T MANY COMIC BOOK ARTISTS AROUND BUT WE STILL GOT TO GET THE GOOD STUFF CHEAP!! OKAY, DREAMER.... SO, WHAT'S THE ANSWER?

AN IN-SHOP STAFF!

THAT WILL MEAN A BIGGER OFFICE!

ILLUSTRATORS! WE'LL PAY SALARIES. THEY ALL DREAM OF A STEADY INCOME ...AND COMIC BOOKS CAN PROVIDE THAT!

WELL, **LEW**... HOW DO YOU **LIKE** WORKING WITH OUR JAPANESE BRUSHES? I CAN USE 'EM, FINE!

OH, THEY'RE OKAY...NOT VERY RESILIENT BUT I CAN HANDLE IT!

AAAAH THEY'RE **CHEAPER!** THAT'S WHY Y' WANT US TO USE THEM!

BET LEW CAN DRAW A **FINER** LINE THAN YOU, BILLY!

IN A SHOP LIKE THIS DRAWING SKILLS AND TECHNIQUE **DOMINATE!** COMPANY-PROVIDED STORIES AND IDEAS DO NOT SATISFY THE ARTISTS' NEED FOR IDENTITY!

YEAH... LET'S HAVE A **DUEL!!** DRAW A FINE LINE, BILLY!

SURE, HERE!

...AND THEN EACH OF YOU KEEP GOING OVER THAT LINE...THE FIRST GUY WHO MAKES IT **THICKER** LOSES... OKAY?

OKAY!

WHEW... I **GIVE UP!!** I BLEW IT...

...LIKE A SURGEON... ATABOY, LEW!

SO MUCH FOR THE BOSS, HAHA, HA

BO BOWERS COMES FROM A FACTORY CITY UPSTATE... HE GREW UP IN A HOME OF CONSERVATIVE CHURCH-GOING EASTERN EUROPEAN IMMIGRANT WORKING CLASS PEOPLE... THERE, DISCIPLINE WAS MIXED WITH TRADITIONAL PREJUDICES. HE WANTS TO ASSIMILATE. HE'S VERY PATRIOTIC! HE CAME TO NEW YORK TO MAKE IT IN THE BIG CITY... HERE, HE CAN FEEL QUITE SUPERIOR TO OTHER IMMIGRANTS. HE'S A GRADUATE OF A BIG ART SCHOOL AND PREFERS REALISM IN ART... FANTASY IS NOT FOR HIM. HE'D RATHER WORK WITH REAL SITUATION STORIES AND 'PRACTICAL' PLOTS.

"...YOU ALRIGHT, BO?

WHAT DID I SAY, ANYHOW?

BO... YOU JUST STUCK A PIN IN A DREAM BUBBLE AND IT BURST IN YOUR FACE!

...HO HUM, ANY BODY FOR A BEER AFTER WORK?

SURE!

SURE!

'NIGHT, BILLY.

NIGHT.

HEY, BILLY... KING, SHARP AND BOWERS ARE GOING OUT FOR A BEER. ...WANT TO COME ALONG?

OH... NO THANKS, ANDREA, I DON'T THINK THEY WANT ME AROUND WHEN THEY GRIPE ABOUT E & S.

I'D LIKE YOU AROUND... SO, HOW ABOUT BUYING ME A DRINK?

WELL, SURE!

85

Annotations to
The Dreamer

by Denis Kitchen

Page 53. The January 21, 1937, date on the *New York Times* at the very opening is a bit misleading. The earliest events in *The Dreamer* occur from 1934 to 1936.

Pages 55–56. The "publisher of cartoon books" approaching young **"Billy"** (**Will Eisner**) was producing small horizontal-shaped booklets depicting pornographic versions of famous newspaper comic strips, such as "Popeye" and "Bringing Up Father." Commonly called eight-pagers or Tijuana Bibles, these inexpensive parodies, much like bootlegged booze, were popular underground items in the 1930s. Because these salacious  booklets violated copyright and trademark laws, they were typically Mafia-distributed ("Giannini family") and sold under the counter by shifty retailers or the type of street vendor humorously associated with a long pocket-lined trench coat.

Page 57. Billy describes the "new comic books" on display as "reprints of daily strips," an accurate description of the earliest comic books, which capitalized on the huge popularity of

newspaper comic strips. Eisner believed that there would soon be a strong market for comic books comprised of original material, which became the basis of his first business success.

Page 59. Eisner's full pseudonym is revealed as **Billy Eyron**. His last name is a nod to Cat Yronwode (pronounced "iron-wood"), itself ironically a pseudonym for Cathy Manfredi. Yronwode was a serious comics fan and editor who helped Eisner organize his archives in the early 1980s. She wrote columns and helped edit Kitchen Sink Press's *Spirit Magazine* and early *Spirit* comic books and she was also one of Will's sounding boards for graphic novel ideas.  They later became estranged but this was Eisner's way of giving her a public tip of his hat in 1986.

The **Pumice Handsoap** ad that the teenage Billy sold for $15 was in reality an ad for **Gre-Solvent**, one of Eisner's first commercial jobs.

Pages 59–60. Ken Corn is **Bob Kane** (originally Kahn). Eisner and Kane attended New York's DeWitt Clinton High School together and they even occasionally double-dated. Kane would soon attain fame as the creator of *Batman*.

Page 60. *Socko: The Fun Magazine* that Ken refers Billy to is *Wow! What a Magazine!*, a short-lived publication edited by **Samuel "Jerry" Iger** (**Jimmy Samson**). The **Henry Fabric Co.** refers to the fact that *Wow!* was a sidebar operation of entrepreneur **John Henle**, whose primary business was manufacturing shirts.

Page 61. Samson's remark, "Did you see how 'Famous Funnies' is selling?" refers to the pioneering *Famous Funnies*, which successfully launched the mushrooming comic book industry in 1934. As the title implies, it reprinted many of the country's best-known syndicated comic strips, such as "Mutt & Jeff" and "Tailspin Tommy," something the low-budget *Wow!* could not effectively compete against.

Page 63. The **"Hawk"** page on Billy's drawing board is **"Hawks of the Seas,"** an early Eisner buccaneer epic, but it is shown here prematurely in a context suggesting that "Hawks of the Seas" was intended to be Eisner's initial contribution to *Wow!* In fact, Eisner contributed a different buccaneer strip to *Wow!* called "The Flame" (which later evolved into "Hawks") along with

"Harry Karry," a humorous detective strip, during the publication's four-issue run.

Page 64. The new comic book packaging company, **Eyron & Samson**, is of course **Eisner & Iger.**

Page 65. Eisner & Iger Studio began business modestly in a tiny office at 43rd and Madison Avenue. When Samson says, "Not much room in here," he's not kidding. Eisner described the dimensions of their first office as approximately ten feet by ten feet.

Page 66. Mr. O'Brien's **Pulpo Publishing Co.** is Thurman T. Scott's **Fiction House Publishing**, an early and important Eisner & Iger client. Fiction House produced pulp magazines like *Fight Stories*, *Planet Stories* and *Jungle Stories*, genres that quickly translated into the newly popular comic book format as audiences for their text-dominated pulps faded. One of Eisner's more famous creations, **"Sheena, Queen of the Jungle,"** was initially created for *Wags*, but the sexy "female Tarzan" made its first big splash in Scott's *Jumbo Comics*, which hit newsstands in the summer of 1938.

Pages 67–69. The colorful **Donald Harrifield** is **Harry Donenfeld,** whose savvy accountant was **Yacov "Jack" Liebowitz (Jakob Lovecraft).** Donenfeld, who owned a printing company (Donny Press) and a distribution company (Independent News), had his eye on National Allied Publications, Inc., a vulnerable publishing customer of both his companies. National Allied (later National Periodicals) was owned by **Major Malcolm Wheeler-Nicholson** (here **Captain Mon-**

trose **B. Wilson**). "The major," as he was called, from his active cavalry officer days, was a successful pulp writer who originated the idea of new editorial content in comic books in 1935. He published *New Fun Comics*, *More Fun Comics* and *Detective Comics*  (the source of the later DC Comics trademark). Conventional wisdom is that Wheeler-Nicholson was a flamboyant character known to sport a beaver hat, Chesterfield coat or French officer's cloak, spats, a cigarette holder and a cane. Having fallen behind in printing and other bills he allegedly lost his company when Donenfeld accepted the major's publishing assets in lieu of printing debts. This scene is Eisner's reenactment of that transaction. On page 68 Eisner depicts the diminutive Donenfeld, on the verge of squeezing out the major, as first having the "dream" to become a publisher. This is not historically accurate. Donenfeld had already been publishing girlie and crime pulps for some years prior to taking over the major's comic book business.

Eisner also depicts Wheeler-Nicholson as another "dreamer" who appears happy to be bought out by his enterprising printer so he can return to writing pulps. Rumors linger, however, that the major was in fact bilked out of his publishing company. When asked why he wasn't harder on Donenfeld and Liebowitz, Eisner replied that he did not know "first hand" that anything underhanded took place, though it was long the publishing industry's dirty little secret that periodicals distribution was a mob-controlled enterprise. Shortly before Will Eisner's death, Gerard Jones's book, *Men of Tomorrow: Geeks, Gangsters and the Birth of the Comic Book*, confirmed the links between Donenfeld and underworld elements and asserted that Wheeler-Nicholson's publishing assets were unfairly granted to Donenfeld in early 1938 by a judge who was a Tammany Hall "buddy" of Donenfeld's. The major litigated in a futile effort to reclaim his company. Wheeler-Nicholson's family vigorously disputes the comics industry's perception of the major, including even the "myth" that he wore flamboyant attire. A forthcoming book by a Wheeler-Nicholson descendent promises to provide yet another side to the sordid and hotly contested origins of the comic book industry.

Pages 70–71. Chuck Maxwell is **Maxwell C. Gaines**. Gaines is generally credited with bringing **Superman** (**Bighero**) to DC Comics in early 1938, though correspondence shows that Wheeler-Nicholson was familiar with *Superman* as early as October 1935. The major had already hired writer **Jerry Siegel** and artist **Joe Shuster** (the "two kids from Ohio")  to do other features for his company such as "Henri Duval" and "Dr. Occult" for *New Fun* and "Slam Bradley" for *Detective Comics*. Eisner fails to mention in *The Dreamer* (though he often laughed about it publicly) that his studio also had the opportunity to acquire *Superman* but rejected it because they felt it was too amateurish. M. C. Gaines's parting words in *The Dreamer,* "Some day soon . . . I'll put out my own books," is a reference to the fact that after forming the All-American comics line in partnership with Donenfeld he broke away from National Periodicals/DC Comics to form Educational Comics, which his son Bill subsequently inherited and transformed into the legendary Entertaining Comics (E.C. Comics) line, which included *MAD* (ironically eventually absorbed by DC Comics). Harrifield's parting comment about the ownership stamp (a mini work-for-hire agreement) on the backs of company checks payable to creators alludes to the fact that the company, like its competitors, owned all rights to the properties it published. Like Wheeler-Nicholson before them, Siegel and Shuster (and their heirs) litigated over the course of many years in an effort to reclaim *Superman,* a property that earned countless millions for DC Comics and later its parent company Time Warner.

Page 72. Eisner's former schoolmate **Bob Kane (Ken Corn)** was one of the first freelancers hired by Eisner & Iger. Kane produced the funny animal filler **"Peter Pupp"** (**"Puppy Dawg")** for the studio. His big costumed hero sale to Harrifield, **"Rodentman,"** is **Batman**, DC's other flagship superhero, alongside Superman.

Page 73. The British comic weekly **"Doggy"** is actually *Wags,* where some of Eisner's earliest work like "Hawks of the Seas" appeared.

Page 74. Lew Sharp is **Lou Fine**, a graduate of Pratt Institute whose draftsmanship Eisner and his associates particularly admired.

Page 76. Illustrator **Armand Budd** is **Alex Blum** while scriptwriter **Andrea Budd** is his daughter **Toni Blum**, the only female in the bullpen.

Page 77. Gar Tooth is **George Tuska,** a normally reserved artist who demonstrated that he had a boiling point.

Page 78. The legendary **Jack "King" Kirby** has the least disguised pseudonym in *The Dreamer,* **Jack King**, though to confuse matters Kirby's birth name was **Jacob Kurtzberg** (which "Bo Bowers" refers to as **Klingensteiner**) and his Eisner & Iger Studio nom de plume was **Jack Curtis**. Kirby went on to great acclaim as the cocreator of Captain America (with Joe Simon) and cocreator (with Stan Lee) of many other Marvel Comics superheroes such as Fantastic Four, Thor, The Hulk and X-Men.

Pages 79–82 Bo Bowers is **Bob Powell** (real name Stanislaus Pawlowski). He drew the early **"Sheena, Queen of the Jungle" ("Jungle Girl")** stories, among many others. Of Polish Catholic ancestry, Powell was one of the few non-Jews in the shop and openly anti-Semitic. A flagrant womanizer, his outspokenness wasn't limited to ethnic slurs. On page 81, where Powell is soundly decked by George Tuska, Eisner pulls his punches even if Tuska doesn't. Tuska, like Eisner (see pages 83–84), had a crush on office mate Toni Blum but was too shy to make his move.

The actual provocation that inflamed Tuska, Eisner privately said, was Powell's loud assertion that he "could fuck [Toni Blum] anytime" he wanted. After decking Powell, Tuska stood

over his prostrate coworker and in a voice Eisner described as Lon Chaney Jr. in *Of Mice and Men* said, "You shouldn't ought to have said that, Bob."

Pages 82–84. The unrequited romance between Eisner and Toni Blum was consistent with Eisner's ready admission that he was "all work and no play" during his early career.

Pages 85–93. The BIGHERO: MAN OF IRON poster is another allusion to Superman, whose nickname is the "Man of Steel." Donenfeld's confident statement that "Bighero is selling out on the stands" is no idle boast. *Superman*, launched in 1938, had already reached sales of a million copies per bimonthly issue by 1939, inviting all manner of hungry entrepreneurs to copy DC's success. The self-interested and "pushy" bookkeeper at DC, **Vincent Reynard**, is **Victor Fox**, who used insider information to set up his own rival company, Fox Feature Syndicate. Fox's **Heroman,** a blatant imitation of Bighero, was **Wonder Man**, a Superman competitor that was very short-lived thanks to Eisner's testimony in court.

Page 94–95. Eisner participated in a career-turning meeting in the autumn of 1939. Though never named here, the meeting led to the creation of Eisner's legendary feature *The Spirit* (1940–52). It was not only a creatively innovative strip but one in an unprecedented format: a 16-page comic book section inserted into subscribing Sunday newspapers. **Mike Henny** of the **"Old-Line" Newspaper Syndicate** is **Henry Martin** of the Des Moines based **Register and Tribune Syndicate**, while **Beansy Everett** is **Everett "Busy" Arnold**, owner of the Quality Comics line. Arnold, shown knocking back drinks while referring to Billy as "a sober . . . kid," was a reputed alcoholic but soon to be Eisner's new partner.

Page 96. Eisner sold his half of Eisner & Iger Studios for $20,000 in late 1939. While that amount was not exactly peanuts during the Great Depression, it was indeed "cheap" considering the track record and success of the Eisner & Iger shop. One factor in the sale not clear in *The Dreamer* is that Eisner did not like Iger personally. But Billy's explanation to Samson is also true; Eisner was indeed eager to create his own strip for an older audience, and newspaper syndication was a much more prestigious and potentially remunerative business than packaging for the lowly regarded comic book field. Eisner, despite being only twenty-two when he entered into his agreement with Arnold and the syndicate, was able to negotiate ownership of *The Spirit*, something unheard of at this time. Even such well-established stars of syndicated newspaper strips like **Al Capp** (*Li'l Abner*) and **Milton Caniff** (*Steve Canyon*) did not acquire ownership of their own strips until the late 1940s (making big news when they did), and the vast majority of syndicated cartoonists never owned their own creations. Even today syndicate ownership is commonplace.

Page 97. Bob Powell, Lou Fine, Chuck Mazoujian (Chuck Mann) and other artists joined the new studio Eisner created following his association with publisher Busy Arnold. Eisner was personally responsible for writing and drawing "The Spirit" portion of the sixteen-page  section he had to deliver weekly to the syndicate. His own story initially comprised eight (later seven) of the sixteen pages. Powell was tapped to do the four-page "Mr. Mystic" back-up feature while Mazoujian was the initial artist on the other back-up feature, "Lady Luck." Artists Jack Cole, Lou Fine and Joe Kubert ghosted "The Spirit" during Eisner's army years in World War II.

to The HEART of the STORM

Introduction to
To The Heart of the Storm

I grew up in the safety of America during the brewing of the storm that culminated in World War II. It was a voyage through a time of social awakenings and pervading concern with economic survival. At the same time, one could hear the rumblings and feel the shock waves from the distant Holocaust.

When I began work on this book, I intended to deliver a narrowly focused fictional experience of that climate, but in the end, it metamorphosed into a thinly disguised autobiography. In such a work, fact and fiction became blended with selective recall and result in a special reality. I came to rely on the truthfulness of visceral memory.

Perhaps the most indelible of my memories of those years was the insidious prejudice that permeated my world. Revisiting it brought me to the realization that primal prejudice has different meanings. To other than whites, it is racism; to the ethnically different, it is nationalism; to Jews, it is anti-Semitism.

This book, completed in the 90th year of the Twentieth Century, documents my coming of age into the dawn of what is generally regarded as a new era. From its beginnings, America managed to sustain and advance the dream of cultural and racial integration. America likes to see itself now as the world's champion of human rights. In these times, more African Americans unapologetically describe themselves by the color of their skin; Hispanics proudly display their culture and language, and young Jews boldly appear in the streets wearing a badge of their faith, the yarmulke. There are acknowledged civil rights, anti-discrimination laws, interfaith forums, intermarriage and a vigilant free press that quickly publicizes racial incidents.

Whether all this is proof of a new prejudice-free world, or simply evidence that the same old hatreds are still within us, is arguable. I cling to the hope that kids growing up today can no longer easily assume a social superiority with its license to discriminate.

But, just in case this view is not too sanguine, I share with you my journey To the heart of the Storm.

Will Eisner

Florida, 1990

IT WAS A TIME OF THUNDER AND LIGHTNING. THE WAR THAT HAD RAVAGED EUROPE SINCE 1939 NOW ENGULFED AMERICA. THERE WORLD WAR II SET IN MOTION THE DRAFTING OF ITS CITIZENS FOR MILITARY SERVICE. YOUNG MEN REGISTERED WITH THEIR LOCAL DRAFT BOARDS.

THERE THEY WERE CLASSIFIED FOR SERVICE. THOSE SELECTED WERE TOLD TO REPORT TO RECRUITING POINTS WHERE THEY WERE EXAMINED, INDUCTED AND ASSIGNED TO BRANCHES. THEY WERE THEN UNIFORMED, GROUPED, AND HERDED ONTO TROOP TRAINS

COMMANDEERED FOR SHIPPING SOLDIERS TO UNANNOUNCED DESTINATIONS. FOR THESE YOUNG PEOPLE IT WAS AN UNFORGETTABLE JOURNEY TO A NEW LIFE. BEHIND THEM WERE THE YEARS OF THEIR YOUTH AND THE

TIME OF GROWING UP. ABOARD THE TRAINS THAT SNAKED ALONG THE RIVERBEDS, SOMBER RECRUITS STARED OUT OF THE GRIMY WINDOWS. IT WAS A TIME TO REFLECT, TO TAKE INVENTORY, NOT AS DYING MEN—FOR THEY HAD STILL TO FACE THAT—BUT RATHER TO SHORE

UP THEIR STRENGTH AGAINST WHAT LAY AHEAD. THEY KNEW INSTINCTIVELY THAT THEIR VALUES AND PREJUDICES WOULD SOON BE TESTED AND THAT PERHAPS NOT AGAIN IN THE RUSH OF LIVING WOULD THERE BE SUCH A MOMENT AS THIS.

115

125

129

132

133

139

141

TOMORROW I'LL GO SEE MY SISTER, ROSE! HER HUSBAND HAS A NEWSPAPER STAND DOWNTOWN... MAYBE HE'LL LET YOU SELL PAPERS, AFTER SCHOOL... IT'S GOOD MONEY, I HEAR!

SELL NEWSPAPERS? ME?? AWW, MA!

... DON'T COMPLAIN! AT LEAST IT'S NOT CHARITY... YOU ARE GOING TO LEARN WHAT IT IS TO MAKE A LIVING... IF YOUR FATHER WASN'T SUCH A BIG SHOT, HE'D DO HOUSE PAINTING WHERE HE REALLY BELONGS!

LET ME TELL YOU... I KNOW FROM EXPERIENCE... LIFE IS NOT EXACTLY PERFECT... YOU HAVE TO DO WITH WHAT YOU ARE GIVEN... FOR ME IT WAS NEVER EASY... NEVER....

NEW YORK
1880

MY FATHER, ISAAC WOLF,
CAME TO AMERICA...I DON'T
REMEMBER WHEN EXACTLY...
COULD BE 1880...IT'S NOT
IMPORTANT...
HE CAME FROM RUMANIA
AND HE BROUGHT WITH HIM
HIS WIFE AND THEIR THREE
CHILDREN: IRVING, MIKE,
AND ROSE.

ISAAC BECAME A TRAVELLING SALESMAN.
HE WAS ALWAYS AWAY FROM HOME. OH,
FOR HIM THAT WAS FINE. HE, ALL THE TIME,
LIKED TO MAKE NEW FRIENDS...
ESPECIALLY LADIES.

143

BUT ISAAC'S WIFE DIED, OF THE FLU, I THINK ...
WHICH IN THOSE DAYS WAS VERY COMMON.''
BY THEN ISAAC WOLF WAS 70 YEARS OLD.

SO, RIGHT AWAY ISAAC WENT BACK TO RUMANIA
TO MARRY HIS WIFE'S YOUNGER SISTER AND BROUGHT
HER OVER. NOT ONLY WAS IT THE **RIGHT** THING TO DO -
ACCORDING TO OUR CUSTOM - BUT HE NEEDED
SOMEONE TO TAKE CARE OF HIS KIDS!

HOO-HAH!'...FATHER WAS A VIGOROUS MAN FOR HIS
AGE...SO ON THE BOAT COMING OVER WITH HIS NEW WIFE,
I WAS BORN!

BY THE TIME ISAAC WOLF REACHED 80, MY MOTHER HAD TWO MORE CHILDREN BY HIM. WE DIDN'T SEE HIM MUCH. HE JUST CAME HOME TO MAKE BABIES — LITTLE ELSE. IT SEEMED TO ME HE DIDN'T GET OLDER LIKE OTHER MEN. SOON, THERE WERE SIX KIDS IN THE HOUSE... IRVING, MIKE, AND ROSE FROM HIS FIRST WIFE AND ME, GOLDIE, AND BOBBY FROM THE NEW ONE.

MOTHER WAS A SICKLY WOMAN AND TAKING CARE OF ALL THOSE KIDS WAS KILLING HER.

ON MY TENTH BIRTHDAY, MY MOTHER DIED.

ALSO THAT YEAR ISAAC WOLF DIED SOMEWHERE ON THE ROAD.

SO THE FAMILY BROKE APART. THERE WERE NO RELATIVES TO TAKE US IN. EVERYBODY HAD THEIR OWN TROUBLES IN THOSE DAYS.

IRVING
THE OLDEST AND THE SMARTEST, GOT A JOB HELPING OUT TELEPHONE MEN SO HE COULD KEEP GOING TO SCHOOL. HE WAS VERY VERY INDEPENDENT SO RIGHT AWAY HE GOT A ROOM FOR HIMSELF.

MIKE
LEFT SCHOOL EARLY AND WENT TO WORK AS A WAITER. HE WAS SICKLY AND A WEAK PERSON.

MY GOD! WHAT AM I GOING TO DO WITH YOU?!

ROSE
WAS NOW ALL WE HAD!! THERE WAS NO CHOICE... IT WAS HER OR THE STREETS.

ROSE WAS A STRONG PERSON. SHE COULD ALWAYS THINK QUICKER THAN EVERYONE! SO, FIRST, SHE PUT BOBBY, THE YOUNGEST, OUT. SHE PAID A FAMILY TO TAKE HIM IN...

...WHICH DIDN'T LAST LONG I CAN TELL YOU!! VERY SOON HE RAN AWAY...LIVING, GOD KNOWS WHERE, IN THE STREETS WITH BUMS AND WORSE!

...THEN SHE PLACED GOLDIE WITH A CHARITY...I DON'T REMEMBER WHICH OR WHAT RELIGION, EVEN. BUT THEY GAVE HER A PLACE TO SLEEP AND WHAT TO EAT!! FOR THIS SHE HELPED OUT WITH THE OLD PEOPLE.

ME, SHE LET LIVE WITH HER! ROSE WORKED BY DAY IN SIEGEL'S FACTORY AND TOOK HOME PIECEWORK AT NIGHT. I HELPED OUT PICKING UP YARD GOODS AND DELIVERING THE FINISHED WORK FOR HER.

BUT ROSE WAS LOOKING FOR A MAN!! SHE WAS A VERY GOOD LOOKING GIRL WITH A NICE FIGURE. MEN NOTICED HER!

...ALSO SHE WAS VERY FORWARD! SHE KNEW WHAT SHE WANTED!! SHE COULD PICK AND CHOOSE.

ROSE, WHY DID YOU SHOW HIM THE DOOR? HE SEEMED NICE.

I CAN'T STAND HIS TYPE... HE WANTS TO BE THE BOSS!!...WELL, *NOT WITH ME HE CAN'T*!

THEN, ONE DAY...

FANNIE, I WANT YOU TO MEET **LOUIE**! WE'RE **GETTING MARRIED**, ...RIGHT, LOUIE?

RIGHT, ROSE! SURE, SURE.

THE FIRST YEAR THEIR MARRIAGE WENT FINE. HE DIDN'T MIND THAT I LIVED THERE! ...THEY WOULD KISS RIGHT IN FRONT OF ME. THEY WERE VERY MODERN.

...BESIDES, LOUIE MADE A GOOD LIVING. HE HAD A STEADY JOB WORKING AT THE NEWSPAPER AT NIGHT...THEN IN THE AFTERNOON HE SOLD PAPERS ON A STREET STAND, SO THERE WAS PLENTY OF MONEY!

ROSE KEPT A GOOD HOUSE. IT WAS SO CLEAN YOU COULD EAT OFF THE FLOOR

ALL I WANT IS JUST THAT IN **MY HOUSE** THINGS ARE DONE **MY WAY!** IS THAT TOO MUCH TO ASK ??

BUT SOMETHING WAS HAPPENING INSIDE ROSE! THE MORE LOUIE OBEYED HER THE ANGRIER SHE GOT...WHO KNOWS WHY!?

AND I SPENT MY CHILDHOOD IN THAT HOUSE.

151

IN A FEW YEARS I BECAME A WOMAN BEFORE MY TIME! BESIDES HELPING ROSE, I HAD GOLDIE AND BOBBY TO WORRY ABOUT... I GREW UP FAST, BELIEVE ME.

153

FANNIE, I'VE GOT TO TALK TO YOU ABOUT SOMETHING!!

YOU'RE 17 NOW, FANNIE. IT'S TIME YOU PAID YOUR WAY AROUND HERE.

BUT, ROSE, I DO ALL YOUR HOUSEWORK. ISN'T THAT ENOUGH?

I MEAN YOU SHOULD BRING IN SOME **MONEY**... LOUIE'S PAPER IS ON STRIKE NOW!

I'D LIKE TO GET OUT AND WORK...BUT I DON'T HAVE ENOUGH EDUCATION.

SHE WANTS TO GET OUT!!! **DID YOU HEAR THAT**, LOUIE ??!

NOW DON'T BE ANGRY ROSE...I ONLY MEANT...

WHAT'S THE MATTER? **I GIVE YOU A ROOF OVER YOUR HEAD**... WITH FOOD AND CLOTHES YET... **IS THAT NOT GOOD ENOUGH FOR YOU !??**

OH, BUT...

DON'T FIGHT HER, FANNIE, SHE'LL **CHEW** YOU TO BITS, BELIEVE ME!

MAYBE I CAN WORK IN A BAKERY SHOP... NOW **THAT** IS HIGH CLASS !!

HIGH CLASS ?? YOU'RE AN IGNORANT GIRL ...YOU'LL SEW IN SIEGEL'S HAT FACTORY ... MISS HIGH CLASS !

WELL, I WENT TO WORK IN SIEGEL'S FACTORY ! YOU KNOW, I DIDN'T MIND SO MUCH... IT TURNED OUT I WAS A PRETTY GOOD WORKER.

YOU GOT GOLDENER HANDS FANNIE HMM♪♪

HA... IMAGINE **ME**...A GIRL WITH A TRADE, YET !

HEY, FANNIE, YOUR KID SISTER IS OUT HERE... MAKE IT FAST-- I DON'T PAY FOR SOCIAL VISITS !

IT'S BOBBY AGAIN !

SIEGEL'S HATS

SEE... SHIPPING AND RECEIVING

OH, GOLDIE !

159

162

163

168

GO HOME, FANNIE!
BOY... HE'S STUBB-O-RIN
HEY, MIKE, YOU AIN'T GOIN' IN AGAIN ?!
@*# !!

176

183

189

FINALLY, THE NEW BOY. HERE, HOLD THE BABY! I'VE GOT TO FINISH THE SCHNECKEN.

BUT MRS. SCHILLER, I AM AN ART STUDENT, YOU UNDERSTAND! WHEN DO I ASSIST HERR SCHILLER?

HA, HA...

WHEN YOU ASSIST ME, YOU ASSIST MEISTER SCHILLER!!

IN THE MORNING YOU'LL CHOP WOOD FOR THE KITCHEN... THEN YOU'LL SWEEP THE STUDIO.

THEN... IN THE AFTERNOON YOU TAKE CARE OF THE BABY WHILE I COOK SUPPER!

THEN, AT FIVE O'CLOCK, FOR TEN MINUTES, YOU CAN GO INTO THE STUDIO AND LOOK AT MY HUSBAND'S WORK!

BUT DON'T ASK QUESTIONS, ...SCHILLER CAN'T STAND THAT!

AHEM... MISSIS SCHILLER

MEIN GOTT, BOY, CAN'T YOU EVEN DIAPER A BABY?

190

194

198

200

201

203

204

207

208

215

216

217

230

233

238

248

251

254

260

WELL, YOU WERE UP THERE A LONG TIME! HOW'D IT GO? TELL ME!

OHHH ♪♪ IT WENT OKAY! SHE WONT TELL ON US NOW!

WOW WHAT DID YOU DO? C'MON, SPILL IT, P-L-E-A-S-E

SORRY, GENTLEMEN JUST DO NOT TALK ABOUT IT! LET'S GET BACK TO WORK!

WE'RE READY FOR VARNISH.

YEP! I'LL BORROW THE MONEY FROM MY FATHER FOR IT. BE HERE TOMORROW!

ZZZ

ZZZ

HI, BUCK... I GOT HERE EARLY TODAY! AHH I SEE YOUR POP LOANED US THE MONEY FOR THE VARNISH.

...YOU KNOW, WE'D BE SMART TO USE A CHEAPER VARNISH AND HAVE MONEY LEFT OVER FOR BRASS...

WHO ARE YOU TO SAY WHAT WE SHOULD DO ?!

279

285

287

288

SO...I BECOME JEWISH... I GO TO A RABBI AND I DO LIKE HE SAYS.

EVERYTHING I DO... INCLUDE **CIRCUMCISE!** I DID IT ALL — AND SO WE MARRIED!

LAST YEAR, MY SOPHIE **DIED**...SO I MOVE BACK TO MY MOMMA'S HOUSE ON MULBERRY STREET.

YOU KNOW WHAT MY LIFE WAS THERE?? **HELL!!**

BUT MOMMA IS ASHAMED OF ME...HER CATHOLIC FRIENDS AVOID ME!!

LAST MONTH I MEET LUPINA. SHE'S AN ANGEL...I WANT TO MARRY HER...BUT SHE SAYS **NO**...SHE **CAN'T MARRY NO JEW!!**

RELIGION, FAH!! *!*

SO NOW I'M GONNA CHANGE BACK TO A CATHOLIC!

290

309

311

Introduction to
The Name of the Game

Dear Reader:

My name is Abraham Kayn. I am the father of Aron Kayn, my only son. We are very proud of him—and grateful too—because he has married into a very high-class family, the Arnheims, you know. He has lifted us up socially.

First of all, my real name is Kayinsky. I came from a little village in Poland and my wife came from a little place in Holland. We were "Nobodies," poor of course, as were my parents, grandparents and great-great-grandparents. As far back as anybody could remember the Kayinskys were never able to raise themselves up. What can I say? First of all we were never smart or lucky in trade. No, we were never better than our neighbors, so we accepted that the only other way up was by marriage.

And why not? All the stories we grew up with told us this. Whether it was history, Bible stories or fairy tales, it was always the same. A great king or nobleman would offer the hand of his beautiful daughter in marriage to the young man (from the lower classes) who performed a great deed. Generation after generation accepted this as true. Certainly for ordinary people this was a dream because any other way was not so easy.

Of course, in modern times, kings and nobles were replaced by tradesmen who accumulated great wealth and established families of power and social position.

Naturally we knew nothing about what went on in that society. Yes, we heard or believed that they all lived a life of comfort, pleasure and enjoyed the power and influence that comes with plenty of money. People from the upper class were better and happier.

How could one not be? Doesn't financial security, belonging to the best people and giving to charities guarantee a good life?? Absolutely. Marrying into such a class guaranteed living happily ever after.

What can I tell you? Marriage for us was, therefore, a game. There were bad marriages and there were good marriages. Marrying beneath oneself was bad. Marrying outside of your religon or race was worse. However, marrying a rich girl (if you were a boy) or marrying a successful man (if you were a girl) was good.

Above all, the family into which one married was most important. To marry into a socially better family would lift your family up. It would provide "connections" and you would be the envy of one's neighbors, especially when one could refer to one's in-laws on a first name basis.

So we came penniless to America, Americanized our name to Kayn, raised and educated a son who married well and changed everything for us.

Today, we are very well connected.

Yes, marriage is the Name of the Game.

Abraham Kayn

The
ARNHEIM
Family

The Arnheim family was descended from Moses Arnheim, one of the many German Jews who had emigrated to America about two decades before the Civil War.

Wealthy and assimilated, they enjoyed a comfortable inclusion in American Society. By 1890, the Arnheims were a leading family in the dominant East Coast German Jewish social establishment.

The first Jews who sought a haven in the American colonies came from Spain and Portugal via Brazil. They soon became American-ized and were well established by the time the United States became a nation. They were a cultured people who adopted community manners and quickly assimilated. As a group, they remained middle class. The more enterprising, who did not intermarry with gentiles, built important families and within the Jewish community they became the aristocracy . . . an upper class. The Sephardics.

Between 1820 and 1840, an economic depression ravaged Germany and the Austro-Hungarian Empire. This economic trouble increased the already virulent anti-Semitism there and accelerated the flight of the Jews into America.

These new immigrants were a crude and noisy people. But they were intelligent, resourceful and innovative, an ideal trait for life in this big and open country that was often crude and noisy itself but where opportunity was so abundant. The hard-working newcomers thrived. They were Ashkenazis, just one rung below the Sephardics on the Jewish social ladder.

It was among this wave of immigrants that the first Arnheim, Moses, arrived in America.

He was well prepared for the New World for he was well educated and had experience in trade. He came from parents who had built a small but successful clothing shop in northern Germany. While he had to abandon this shop during the pogrom, he nonetheless brought with him the experience that could be used to his advantage in the new environment.

Moses Arnheim was quick to follow immigrant countrymen who rose from peddlers to entrepreneurs, who established factories, stores and banks.

Upon his arrival in New York City, Moses immediately set up a little corset factory downtown. Moses supervised the manufacturing, and during the season traveled from city to city selling to retail shops. In 1850, corsets for women were an essential fashion element and the company grew quickly. Before long, Moses Arnheim was so wealthy he was able to gain acceptance by the established German Jewish merchant princes and bankers like the Straus, Lehman, Goldman, Loeb, Bloomingdale, Morgenthau and Guggenheim families. Moses was socially ambitious and determined to found a family that, as he always put it, "would mean something." He married well and sired three sons who joined the family business. Moses regarded his youngest, Isidore, as the most accomplished of the three. He left him with 52 percent of the stock and control of the company.

When Moses Arnheim died, Isidore inherited a well-established business with a good family name. His brothers produced four children. Three sons joined the company and the daughter "lived off" the family. Isidore joined the best clubs and married Alva Straus from one of the best Jewish families.

Isidore ran Arnheim Corset Company well. But he was less capable at bringing up his own two sons, Alex and Conrad.

322

And so the boys grew up. Alex, a shy and nervous child, lived in the shadow of Conrad, an aggressive boy who was adored by his mother and favored by his father. Nothing was denied Conrad. His path through childhood was smoothed by his doting parents.

The years at Benton slipped by. Conrad had a number of second chances. Finally, his graduation was negotiated and the Arnheim family could boast an academy graduate. Anything else would have been unthinkable in their social circle. Conrad's pre-manhood was typical of the other boys in his set. A year in Europe, vacations in the mountains, tennis, golf, horseback riding and parties, parties, parties.

Suddenly, one day . . .

The OBER *Family*

Not all of the immigrant German Jews remained in the big seaport cities. The more adventurous headed West and settled in the open country where small towns were in need of the enterprise and trading skills Jews had learned in Europe. Two years after the Civil War, Chaim Ober arrived in the riverhead town of Lavolier. Originally a trading post in the Ohio territory, it gradually became a farming community.

Chaim Ober opened a small dry goods store after a few years of peddling throughout the countryside. He could barely speak English, so his son Abner soon took over the management of the store.

Abner was very successful and popular. Eventually the Obers became quite wealthy and a part of Lavolier society. They were a good family.

The Ober home was one of the finest in the lower river valley. The Obers entertained often and their daughter, Lilli, was sought after by all the young swains in town. To marry into the Ober family was a dream shared by many a Jewish mother in Lavolier. They were, after all, the best family.

But the Obers themselves had dreams; privately, they had greater social ambitions.

So they willingly "sat" for local society newspaper feature stories.

Who could resist the prospect of moving up socially? Not even a small-town banker. Most unusual was the ease with which the invitations came. Social inclusion into the upper class German Jewish society was never this easy . . .

Late that summer Lilli left Lavolier for her new life in New York.

So, in the autumn during the High Holy Days, the Obers came to New York . . . not for any religious observance but to meet Isidore Arnheim.

The following two weeks were dazzling for the Obers. They were given a place in the Arnheim pew at temple. They were introduced to people whose social and financial status was awesome.

In New York, Lilli Ober seemed to grow up overnight. Under the Teutonic Arnheim tutelage, the small town girl blossomed into a "suitable" young woman who fit neatly into their society. All the next year, the Arnheims included Lilli in their social program. Not surprisingly, almost every social event included Conrad.

That spring, a letter arrived for the Obers in Lavolier.

THE LAVOLIER COURIER

VOL.5 ISSUE 52   JUNE 19, 1910   TWO CENTS

SOCIETY

OBER–ARNHEIM WEDDING SOCIAL EVENT OF SEASON

The joining of two very prominent families brought to Lavolier two hundred guests from as far away as New York.

The Ober family, leaders of the Jewish community in our city for over two decades, celebrated the wedding of their daughter Lillian to Conrad Arnheim of New York.

Local luminaries who filled the pews of the Beth Shalom Synagogue on Elm Street came from the cream of society.

Mayor Jim Bryan, Senator Owen Hill, Rabbi and Mrs. Alex Ochs, Mr. and Mrs. Stetson, Mr. and Mrs. Cohen.

WEDDING MENU

The reception feast was the season's most sumptuous array of continental cuisine.

Beginning with a light buffet in which French truffles and baby clams were featured, the guests were then served a main course.

Another year passed. While Lilli immersed herself in the Arnheim social world, she enjoyed little, if any, attention from Conrad. Her only comfort was the growing closeness with her father-in-law. She now depended on old Isidore's protection.

After the turn of the century, change seemed to accelerate in America. New technology affected every sector of the country's life. Many of the manufacturing companies established in the Industrial Revolution were aging. Transportation and communication advances made many of the factories that grew out of the Civil War obsolete.

The Arnheim Corset Company had become an institution in the minds of the cousins that formed the Arnheim clan. They all had secure berths in the company. Any changes were resisted and innovation frowned upon. The company always seemed to have run itself. Aggressive selling had come to be regarded as a practice more suitable to a lower class of people.

When Isidore died, the Arnheims lost the strong leadership that had propelled the company. Secure in their social position, they somehow believed they were insulated from the turbulence of the common world of business.

Word traveled quickly in the Arnheim social set. Rumors and gossip about business were of a particular interest, for they were, after all, the underpinnings of status in this world.

351

One of the requirements for maintaining a position in society was to have what others had. It was fundamental to the art of assimilation, the skill of looking like the "haves" and doing what "they" did regardless of one's real interests.

While people like the Arnheims understood the game, it was distasteful to them . . . after all, it was "climbing." But they played it nevertheless.

In Lavolier, news of Lilli's pregnancy brought the Obers up to New York to visit their daughter.

...SUCH GOOD NEWS, LILLI... A GRANDCHILD FOR US! WONDERFUL

OH, MOMMA, POPPA ...IT WAS SUCH A NICE VISIT.

YOU'LL COME DOWN TO LAVOLIER FOR THE HOLIDAYS AFTER THE BABY COMES!

HMMM I DON'T LIKE HOW SHE LOOKS!

OH... SHE'S SAD. HER CONRAD IS ALWAYS... "AWAY" WHO KNOWS WHERE!

ALSO...I HEAR THAT HE NEGLECTS HIS BUSINESS! OUR BANK WON'T LEND TO THE ARNHEIMS ANYMORE.

I DON'T LIKE HOW THE MARRIAGE IS GOING, ABNER!

THAT BOY, CONRAD, NEEDS A TALKING TO!!

I'M GOING TO HAVE A TALK WITH HIS MOTHER.

But the visit with Conrad's mother was fruitless as well as frustrating. The Ober family's values were quite different from those of the Arnheims.

So the Obers returned to Lavolier, where their bank was having a problem with the Arnheim Company loan.

Europe was aflame. The war that was set in motion by an assassination in Serbia seemed so very far away that it was hardly noticed by the Arnheims except, of course, it put a stop to the annual continental tour.

Except for the severe drop in their export sales, the Arnheim Corset Company kept afloat.

But the war eventually spread to America.

America's entrance into the First World War accelerated the fortunes of many companies, but it did just the opposite for the Arnheim interests. Conrad succeeded in avoiding military service, concentrated on his social life, and paid little attention to the company's business except for the mandatory quarterly board meetings.

By the end of the war, the Arnheim Corset Company was foundering.

Within a month of the Arnheim Corset Company failure, Conrad Arnheim bought a seat on the New York Stock Exchange and opened a brokerage firm on Park Avenue. It thrived from the start.

His patronage came from his family's connections and social contacts. The Arnheim name still meant something. After all, who better to entrust one's money to than "one of us." At any rate, the stock market was booming and Conrad could do no wrong.

The infection of financial decay seemed to be spreading to other areas of the Arnheim family. Conrad's cousin Edith Arnheim married Roland Sydney, scion of the famed Sydney Clothing Store family. It was a good marriage socially but an unfortunate choice financially. The Sydney stores went bankrupt soon after the marriage of the young couple, leaving Roland unemployed and broke. His had little beyond his family name.

370

The boom years and the growth of the brokerage business rein-
forced the Arnheim name and Conrad's leadership.

The news of Lilli's difficulty brought Alva home from the spa in Switzerland.

As the doctor feared, Lilli died in childbirth. The Obers, who spent her last days with their daughter, remained after the funeral for an Arnheim and Ober family discussion.

Of course, the Arnheim family prevailed. The Obers returned home and Alva took charge of Helen's care. With her usual determination, she devoted full time and energy to the matter, which left Conrad plenty of freedom to pursue his social life.

But a few months later . . .

It was not difficult to convince the Obers. They were more than willing to take the child and bring her up in Lavolier. They arrived within the week.

This turn of events seemed to finally separate the Ober and the Arnheim families.

Lilli's child was with the Obers. The question of whether she would be brought up as an Ober or an Arnheim was no longer of any consequence.

The alliance, the melding of two good families that would elevate the Obers and strengthen the financial base of the Arnheims, never materialized.

The booming years of the Roaring Twenties was making millionaires by the dozens. The social group that, at one time, had seemed so exclusive was growing. The German Jewish country clubs were beginning to accept a few suddenly wealthy Russian and Polish Jews. Philanthropy was accomplishing social inclusion for the newly rich.

The only delineation left for the good families was that they were "old money." The invaders were merely "new money" and their need to show their affluence by more expensive and showier clothes and goods only made the difference more obvious.

The social standing of the Obers remained unchanged in Lavolier. In New York, the Arnheims managed to keep their good name. While marriage was no longer the only way to a higher social level, big money could still buy status and protect it.

These were good years for Conrad Arnheim. He had money and social position.

So it went until October of 1929.

383

And indeed, appearances *were* kept up!

But the frayed outer edges of the family still had to be dealt with . . .

Along with the early German Jews who wandered westward, Oskar Krause found his way into a small Nebraska town named Cranston. There he learned how to make clay cooking pots. By the time of the Civil War he had built a small but thriving business making and selling ceramic ware. Soon he set up a factory and became a leading citizen in Cranston. By the time he died in 1890 Krause Ceramics was a large thriving company. Oskar was survived by his young gentile wife and a son, David, who took over when she died five years later.

For a while, Krause Ceramics had a virtual monopoly in the area. But as railroads pushed west providing access to the amply capitalized eastern factories, their competition soon overwhelmed the Krause Company and drove it into insolvency. By then, David was part of the Cranston social set and considered a "good catch." In an effort to shore up his finances, he married the daughter of a substantial Jewish grain broker. She soon died. David then married Edna Wein, a local girl from a modest family. He soon squandered the money left to him by his former wife and died broke in 1914, leaving Edna and their infant daughter with little more than the Krause name. His daughter's name was Eva.

Eva was an exceptionally beautiful child. She was adored by her mother, who showed her off at every opportunity. Edna entered Eva in every fair and beauty contest. Sheltered from the usual teenage contacts by a hovering mother, the girl seemed to have few social relations. There was an occasional flirtation, but aside from an attempted rape by a football player, Eva grew up an untouched beauty.

389

Back in Cranston, the news from New York set the town's society abuzz. Edna Wein Krause's daughter was moving in the Arnheim crowd, and the rumors of her glittering social life were supported by her letters. Edna Wein Krause had reason to be proud. It was a social triumph.

All her life Alva Straus Arnheim never had a moment of doubt about the way things were and the way they ought to be in their society. Her marriage to Isidore was exactly as she was taught to expect. There was plenty of money, and her husband's success provided status and stability. The uncertain feeling of being Jewish in a Christian world had dissipated after years of living so securely in America. There was no question about this in the minds of anyone in the social enclave that the Arnheims dominated. Her energy and instinct for control enabled her to maintain a certain leadership during the long years of her widowhood. The family had become a kind of royalty whose position needed constant vigilance and protection.

Strength of character or manipulation were the ways to deal with unsettling events or to monitor the wayward.

But the aging matriarch finally succumbed to the effects of the stroke she had suffered years before.

While Conrad's business was doing well, something was nagging him . . . family! Strangely, with the death of his mother, a sense of family preservation began to occupy his mind.

404

A month later . . .

The custody matter did not "go away" as Conrad hoped and
expected. No Arnheim had ever been threatened like this.

416

The elimination of the Ober claim left Helen firmly settled in the
Arnheim household. Eva began to play the role of "Mother," which
their friends seemed to expect of her. The Arnheims' social schedule
included a lot of "being seen," and for a short time Helen served as a
convenient show piece. But soon their social schedule was so
demanding that Eva began to find it uncomfortable. Because of the
war in Europe, the use of Switzerland, which had long been suitable
as the location of finishing schools for most of the Arnheim set, was
no longer viable. Canada, with its ski resorts, now served a similar
purpose. Eva began to think of this option as a way of relieving herself of Helen's care.

Helen was now in Canada. It left Conrad and Eva alone again. Their world seemed to settle into its normal orbit. Very little changed in their relationship . . . except . . . one night . . .

Two months later

Eva's pregnancy was an easy one and to everyone's surprise, she accepted her new role with the confidence of an actress.

Conrad was delighted and immediately used the event as a celebration.

427

. . . That January . . .
In Canada . . .

Outward appearances, so important to the Arnheims, did not change, but the tragedy had an impact upon the dynamics between Conrad and Eva.

Eva Arnheim was now consolidating control over the family's social position. With Helen's passing, she was free to concentrate on Rosie.

The war's end opened a new era in the stock market. Trading was now becoming more sophisticated. There even were days when a million shares were traded. One or two houses were starting mutual funds, and more pension funds were enlarging their stock portfolios.

The Arnheim Company still catered to small holders—widows, retirees and old-line family estates.

Rosie did well at Wainright, academically. But socially she remained out of the inner circle of student life. Independent and outspoken, she was rarely included socially.

440

So Rosie remained home but went to the school of her choice.

442

445

448

450

POPPA, COME BACK TO THE TABLE!

LET HIM BE, ARON! HE'S SO SENTIMENTAL ABOUT FAMILY.

So this is America, Abe? It is so big... how will we live here?

We were crazy to come here! We have no connections!

Don't worry, Gert, I'm a good painter... there is always work for good house painters... You'll see

It's just that we have no people here

Can I help it if we have no family left?... we must get along the best we can...

Poppa how come we never have any family gatherings like my friends have??

Someday you'll marry and your wife will bring you relatives ...you'll see, Aron

SO, ROSIE, TELL ME...YOU GOT A BIG FAMILY?

455

458

465

Aron's control of the Arnheim Company increased each year. He had mastered the skills necessary to lead the small-investor and widow-dependent firm to a more lucrative estate business. And he was clever enough to keep the company's following alive with the social set that traditionally provided its "bread and butter" income.

This enhanced the relationship between Aron and Conrad. Aron also made a point of keeping Conrad's identity with the company alive, which, of course, pleased Conrad and kept clients.

467

Aron and Rosie's marriage began to reflect the life style Aron thought the business demanded. In an almost magical way, Aron gradually assumed Conrad's style and manner. The Kayns were succumbing to a transformation. More and more, their behavior conformed to the attitudes and mores of their enviroment.

470

471

473

474

479

And that is how the Kayn family was elevated from its lowly station. True, they would always remain an appendage to the prominent Arnheims. But, in the scheme of things, they would enjoy the peripheral social benefits that came from such a connection.

ARNHEIM FAMILY GIVES ONE MILLION TO FUND FOR JEWISH CHARITIES

Rose Arnheim Kayn and her husband Aron, who administer the well-known Arnheim Family Philanthropies, announced their latest annual giving program at a benefit banquet on Tuesday.

The Arnheim estate remains in the forefront of charitable giving in the Jewish community. Aron Kayn, formerly with the Sydney & Arnheim Mutual Fund, now devotes his time to managing

Rose Arnheim Kayn and Aron Kayn with their son Conrad at the recent ball honoring them.

COME IN, GERT! ...THE LADIES ARE EXPECTING YOU!

There was once, in ancient times, a mighty king who ruled a great land which was handed down to him by his parents who so spoiled him that he expected everything to go his way. His first marriage was arranged with the princess of another royal family from a lower kingdom. In time, the couple had a daughter. But the king was uninterested. So when his queen died, he sent the child to live with her grandparents in their kingdom. A few years later, the king remarried a great beauty who did not want children at all. But the king wanted to have a child in his castle so the king had his daughter taken from her grandparents and brought to live with him. When she grew older, the girl found a suitor. She wanted to marry him but the king broke them up simply because the young man was not of royal blood. The daughter was so heartbroken that she died. Later, the king's new wife had a child -- a beautiful and outspoken princess. And it came to pass that a poor, handsome woodworker wandered by one day. The princess fell in love with him. By then the king, guilty about his treatment of his first child, offered his daughter's hand in marriage to the handsome young peasant. They married and the king made him a prince. In time the humble woodworker inherited the crown and became king.

And they lived happily ever after.

THE DAY I BECAME A PROFESSIONAL

Sketches

The following pages showcase some of Will Eisner's preliminary pencil sketches and character studies for his graphic novel *The Name of the Game*. The initial cover concept, the very first drawing in this section, reveals that Eisner's original title was *A Good Marriage*. He obviously changed his mind about the title, but retained the composition for the aborted cover, moving it inside. It remained largely intact as the dramatic opening scene of Aron and Rosie's wedding day (page 453).

The character studies represent Eisner's very first visual conception of the wardrobes and major cast members of *The Name of the Game*. Some of the characters' images ended up evolving. The hair on Aron as a radical young poet, for example, ended up considerably shaggier, and Aron's father ultimately had no glasses and more hair. But for the most part Eisner stuck with his initial gut instinct for each character.

—D.K.

ISIDORE ARNHEIM

HANNAH ARNHEIM

CONRAD ARNHEIM

ALEX ARNHEIM

LILLI OBER

THE OBERS

ABNER OBER

MOTHER OBER

EVA KRAUSE

EVA'S MOTHER

WILLIAMS

CLARA
YOUNG

OLDER

HELEN
YOUNG

ROSE

BABY

SCHOOL

ARON

YOUNG

ARON'S FATHER

ARON'S MOTHER

About the Author

Will Eisner (1917–2005) was the grand old man of comics. He was present at the birth of the comic book industry in the 1930s, creating such titles as *Blackhawk* and *Sheena, Queen of the Jungle*. He created *The Spirit* in 1940, syndicating it for twelve years as a unique and innovative sixteen-page Sunday newspaper insert, with a weekly circulation of 5 million copies. In the seven decades since, *The Spirit* has almost never been out of print. As a Pentagon-based warrant officer during World War Two, Eisner pioneered the instructional use of comics, continuing to produce them for the U.S. Army under civilian contract into the 1970s, along with educational comics for clients as diverse as General Motors and elementary school children.

In 1978 Eisner created the first successful "graphic novel," *A Contract With God*, launching a bold new literary genre. Nearly twenty celebrated graphic novels by him followed. Since 1988 the comic industry's top award for excellence has been "The Eisner." He has received numerous honors and awards worldwide, including, ironically, several Eisners and only the second Lifetime Achievement Award bestowed by the National Foundation for Jewish Culture (2002). Michael Chabon's Pulitzer Prize–winning novel *The Amazing Adventures of Kavalier & Clay* is based in good part on Eisner.